The Mungle Flap

RODERICK HUNT
Pictures by Nigel McMullen

Oxford University Press

We're off to trap the Mungle Flap.
Its eyes glow red and bright.
Its jaws snip snap.
Its wings clip clap.
Its shiny claws go scrip, scrop, scrap.

We’ve got to catch the Mungle Flap,
and bring it home tonight.

So trap, trap the Mungle Flap,
down in its gloomy glen.
We've got to catch the Mungle Flap,
and we won't come home till then.

We've got a trap for the Mungle Flap –
a great big Mungle net.
With ropes that wrap
round a stretchy strap.
It's a very clever sort of trap.

And it's sure to catch the Mungle Flap,
though we haven't used it yet.

So trap, trap the Mungle Flap,
down in its dusty den.
We've got to catch the Mungle Flap,
and we won't come home till then.

And if we catch the Mungle Flap,
we've a special sort of hut.
With an iron grid,
and a screw-down lid.
And no matter what that creature did –

we'd lock the door on the Mungle Flap,
and keep it firmly shut!

So trap, trap the Mungle Flap,
in forest, field or fen.
We've got to catch the Mungle Flap,
and we won't come home till then.

Well! Can this be the Mungle Flap,
with claws that tear and pierce?
It has no growl?
No fearful howl?
It's just a little woodland fowl?

If we have caught the Mungle Flap,
it isn't very fierce!

So clap, clap the Mungle Flap –
it's a useful little hen.
We've got one egg from the Mungle Flap,
and we need another ten!